The Power Of ME

The Rise of An Empowered Empathic Phoenix Leader-preneur (Creation Journal Planner)

AliNICOLE "WATERS"

The Power Of ME

The Power Of ME

It's Time To Rise!!!!!!!!!!!!
You Are A Powerful Phoenix

As an empathic leader-preneur you have superpowers that are far beyond your current view and wildest imagination. Often the illusion of feeling disempowered by high-sensitivity to others, your surroundings and more can distract you and make you feel defeated, burned out or powerless to rise above the situation.

This often effects how you will show up in several areas of your life, leadership and also as an entrepreneur. Let me empower you by saying that you are here to be a powerful influencer and also a demonstrator of true empathic power. The ability to powerfully rise out your own ashes like the mythical bird the Phoenix is an innate superpower that you posses as an empath. Anytime you feel burned out it's a call to rise to a new level of power for your higher service. Anytime you feel like you're being distracted or defeated by any of life's circumstances it's a call to choose the Higher & Lighter way.

This starts with acknowledging that there is a such power within you that can cause you to rise like a Phoenix. Next, you must step into a new

The Power Of ME

level of responsibility to this new power and then you must embrace and embody this new expanded empowered empathic expression.

This is where YOU as a leader-preneur can begin to create a better world for yourself and others starting with your new mission and higher calling to yourself and your service.

Your new empathic success frameworks are born anew from rising into a higher way of BEING-NESS as a leader-preneur. This is how you will start to create the ultimate holistic high-end success experience on the path of the Higher & Lighter way.

The power of YOU is ready to rise with new passions, desires and set forth a new blaze in the world with your newer expanded awareness of empowerment as an empathic leader-preneur.

You are first and foremost not just a leader and entrepreneur, but an accelerated leader and entrepreneur who is empowered and also gifted as an empath to leverage your high-sensitivity to create solutions in your industry and more.

The Power Of ME

Your new calling to RISE HIGH will catapult your success in ways unimaginable. You are the POWERFUL PHOENIX and it's time to rise in the POWER OF YOU!

Allow this creation journal to be the sacred space where you create your NOW & NEXT levels of empowered empathic success for your life and leader-preneurship. Rinse and repeat this process at every new phase as you continue to level up in new power as you RISE HIGHER.

The Power Of ME

Questions to Consider
for Your Journaling Experience

Where am I ready to rise?

What's currently burned up, yet ready to rise anew?

What's the higher service path that is calling me NOW?

What areas of my empathic experience can I leverage my PHOENIX POWER?

What is my Higher & Lighter Way for life and leader-preneurship?

How can I currently rise ANEW?

What am I most passionate about and have a new burning desire for?

What does my new empowered empathic leader-preneur success model look like?

The Power Of ME

I AM A RISEN
Empowered Empathic Phoenix
Creation Journal Section

The Power Of ME

MY RISE IN NEW POWER

Use this section to reflect on the reading and questions. Record your insights and create a new success framework that feels most aligned for you in the present.

The Power Of ME

More Reflections & Creative Planning

I HAVE RISEN MASTER PLAN

The Power Of ME

My New Creation Of ME & More

The Power Of ME

MY ULTIMATE NEW POWER PLAN

The Power Of ME

MY RISE IN NEW POWER

Use this section to reflect on the reading and questions. Record your insights and create a new success framework that feels most aligned for you in the present.

The Power Of ME

More Reflections & Creative Planning

The Power Of ME

I HAVE RISEN MASTER PLAN

The Power Of ME

My New Creation Of ME & More

The Power Of ME

MY ULTIMATE NEW POWER PLAN

The Power Of ME

MY RISE IN NEW POWER

Use this section to reflect on the reading and questions. Record your insights and create a new success framework that feels most aligned for you in the present.

The Power Of ME

More Reflections & Creative Planning

The Power Of ME

I HAVE RISEN MASTER PLAN

The Power Of ME

My New Creation Of ME & More

The Power Of ME

MY ULTIMATE NEW POWER PLAN

The Power Of ME

MY RISE IN NEW POWER

Use this section to reflect on the reading and questions. Record your insights and create a new success framework that feels most aligned for you in the present.

The Power Of ME

More Reflections & Creative Planning

The Power Of ME

I HAVE RISEN MASTER PLAN

The Power Of ME

My New Creation Of ME & More

The Power Of ME

MY ULTIMATE NEW POWER PLAN

The Power Of ME

MY RISE IN NEW POWER

Use this section to reflect on the reading and questions. Record your insights and create a new success framework that feels most aligned for you in the present.

The Power Of ME

More Reflections & Creative Planning

The Power Of ME

I HAVE RISEN MASTER PLAN

The Power Of ME

My New Creation Of ME & More

The Power Of ME

MY ULTIMATE NEW POWER PLAN

The Power Of ME

MY RISE IN NEW POWER

Use this section to reflect on the reading and questions. Record your insights and create a new success framework that feels most aligned for you in the present.

More Reflections & Creative Planning

I HAVE RISEN MASTER PLAN

The Power Of ME

My New Creation Of ME & More

The Power Of ME

MY ULTIMATE NEW POWER PLAN

The Power Of ME

MY RISE IN NEW POWER

Use this section to reflect on the reading and questions. Record your insights and create a new success framework that feels most aligned for you in the present.

The Power Of ME

More Reflections & Creative Planning

I HAVE RISEN MASTER PLAN

The Power Of ME

My New Creation Of ME & More

The Power Of ME

MY ULTIMATE NEW POWER PLAN

The Power Of ME

MY RISE IN NEW POWER

Use this section to reflect on the reading and questions. Record your insights and create a new success framework that feels most aligned for you in the present.

More Reflections & Creative Planning

The Power Of ME

I HAVE RISEN MASTER PLAN

The Power Of ME

My New Creation Of ME & More

The Power Of ME

MY ULTIMATE NEW POWER PLAN

The Power Of ME

MY RISE IN NEW POWER

Use this section to reflect on the reading and questions. Record your insights and create a new success framework that feels most aligned for you in the present.

More Reflections & Creative Planning

The Power Of ME

I HAVE RISEN MASTER PLAN

The Power Of ME

My New Creation Of ME & More

MY ULTIMATE NEW POWER PLAN

The Power Of ME

MY RISE IN NEW POWER

Use this section to reflect on the reading and questions. Record your insights and create a new success framework that feels most aligned for you in the present.

The Power Of ME

More Reflections & Creative Planning

The Power Of ME

I HAVE RISEN MASTER PLAN

The Power Of ME

My New Creation Of ME & More

The Power Of ME

MY ULTIMATE NEW POWER PLAN

The Power Of ME

MY RISE IN NEW POWER

Use this section to reflect on the reading and questions. Record your insights and create a new success framework that feels most aligned for you in the present.

More Reflections & Creative Planning

I HAVE RISEN MASTER PLAN

The Power Of ME

My New Creation Of ME & More

The Power Of ME

MY ULTIMATE NEW POWER PLAN

The Power Of ME

MY RISE IN NEW POWER

Use this section to reflect on the reading and questions. Record your insights and create a new success framework that feels most aligned for you in the present.

The Power Of ME

More Reflections & Creative Planning

The Power Of ME

I HAVE RISEN MASTER PLAN

The Power Of ME

My New Creation Of ME & More

The Power Of ME

MY ULTIMATE NEW POWER PLAN

The Power Of ME

MY RISE IN NEW POWER

Use this section to reflect on the reading and questions. Record your insights and create a new success framework that feels most aligned for you in the present.

The Power Of ME

More Reflections & Creative Planning

I HAVE RISEN MASTER PLAN

The Power Of ME

My New Creation Of ME & More

The Power Of ME

MY ULTIMATE NEW POWER PLAN

MY RISE IN NEW POWER

Use this section to reflect on the reading and questions. Record your insights and create a new success framework that feels most aligned for you in the present.

The Power Of ME

More Reflections & Creative Planning

The Power Of ME

I HAVE RISEN MASTER PLAN

The Power Of ME

My New Creation Of ME & More

The Power Of ME

MY ULTIMATE NEW POWER PLAN

The Power Of ME

MY RISE IN NEW POWER

Use this section to reflect on the reading and questions. Record your insights and create a new success framework that feels most aligned for you in the present.

The Power Of ME

More Reflections & Creative Planning

The Power Of ME

I HAVE RISEN MASTER PLAN

The Power Of ME

My New Creation Of ME & More

The Power Of ME

MY ULTIMATE NEW POWER PLAN

The Power Of ME

MY RISE IN NEW POWER

Use this section to reflect on the reading and questions. Record your insights and create a new success framework that feels most aligned for you in the present.

More Reflections & Creative Planning

The Power Of ME

I HAVE RISEN MASTER PLAN

The Power Of ME

My New Creation Of ME & More

The Power Of ME

MY ULTIMATE NEW POWER PLAN

The Power Of ME

More Related Resources
Visit:
www.thepowerofmyinnerphoenix.tumblr.com
www.bornanewphoenix.blogspot.com

Follow New Definition Empaths
on Facebook

Request to Join
Emerging Empathic-preneurs
Facebook Group

Visit the Author's Amazon Page
www.amazon.com/author/alicianwaters

To Book the Author for
Speaking Engagements
Email:
anwempires@gmail.com

If you enjoyed this resource, please feel free to leave a positive review on Amazon.
Thanks So Much

The Power Of ME